The Yearning Tree

A Children's Bereavement Resource

by Gina Farago

Photographs by Karl Farago

KG Haven Press

www.theyearningtree.net

Published by KG Haven Press
www.theyearningtree.net

ISBN 978-0-615-41485-0

Printed in the U.S.A.

Special thanks to:

Meghan Davis, former Kids Path Assistant Director with Hospice and Palliative Care of Greensboro, NC; fellow counselors Laura Crawford, Jenny Prevatt, Liz Raygor, Katie Thomas; and social worker Kate Hubbard

Kathryn Nider Wolf, MEd., Associate Professor of Early Childhood Education, Guilford Technical Community College, Jamestown, NC

Barbara S. Bane, Editor, Consultant, and Cat Wrangler

T. Glenn Bane, Award-Winning Artist, Author, and Indie Designer

Cynthia Moore Brown, Folkteller, Author, and Educational Consultant

David and Evelyn Moore

Mr. Matthew D. Weaver, Nine-Year-Old Extraordinaire

For all our loved ones who have moved on...

The Yearning Tree was written for children who have lost a loved one or are being affected by someone else's grief. One of the hardest things about grieving is knowing how to talk about it, and for children, this is especially difficult. This book facilitates conversation about feelings and encourages thoughtful discussion through developmentally appropriate questions located in the back.

The purpose of this book is no accident. My personal journey on the "grief walk" has taken me to many places, some dark and sad, some spiritual and full of hope. On this journey, I became a Hospice volunteer, surrounding myself with amazing people who understand the complexity of emotions that mourning presents. I learned a lot in a brief period of time, not about death, surprisingly, but about life. This book is a result of those experiences...in both coping with my own personal bereavement and by being exposed to those dealing with the sorrow of others.

I hope you enjoy this simple story of Maggie and Skittles, two friends on different sides of the grief walk, who find enlightenment and joy again at the end of it.

Gina Farago

$\mathcal{B}$lue misted mountains rose up behind them. Green, grassy pastures carpeted the valley below. Bright butterflies and dandelion drifted on the breeze all around. Life was happy on the farm, and Maggie and Skittles, the two dogs who lived there, just loved it.

But then, one day, everything changed.

"It happened on a Monday," explained Skittles, Maggie's tiniest and dearest fuzzy friend. "Such an ordinary day to lose all our laughter. One minute we were playing, running, doing all the things we always do on the farm.

"The next minute, Maggie was up there, under the tree. She sits there like that all day, staring at it, wishing for her friend Sammy to come back. He was buried there, on what started out as that most ordinary day.

"I have a name for the tree. The tree where Maggie sits and stares and spends her days. I call it...

"...the Yearning Tree."

"Maggie! Maggie!" Skittles bounded up the hill to her friend. "Come down to the woods today! There are squirrels to chase and rabbits to catch."

Maggie turned her head toward the tiny poodle. She sniffed loudly. "Rabbits to catch? And what would you do with a rabbit if you caught it, little one?"

Skittles puffed up, making herself as big and mighty as she could. "I...I..." Skittles fell silent. The thought had never occurred to her before. Just what would she do with a rabbit?

"Go away, little Skittles. I am too tired to play with you today." Maggie swished her tail and turned to look at the tree once more.

Skittles went back down the hill to the barn. The barn manager, Wise Cat, lived there, high on his hunting perch in the windowsill. He would surely know what to do with a rabbit and all the mice on the farm besides. But it was not rabbits or mice that worried Skittles. It was Maggie.

"Don't pounce, Wise Cat! It's only me, Skittles."

"Hmph. So it is." Cat jumped down, looking rather disappointed. He settled in the grass to nap. Finally, when Skittles didn't go away, he opened one owlish eye just a slit and asked, "Something troubles you?"

"Maggie will not play with me. She will not eat. She sits and stares at that tree all day."

"The tree where Sammy is buried." Cat's green eye glittered as he spoke. "Sammy was her good friend, just as Maggie is yours. But he is gone now. Do you understand this?"

Skittles cocked her head from side to side. "Gone where? Into the ground? Into the tree?"

Cat smiled, as much as a cat could smile, and said, "No. Only his body is there. But his spirit," Cat looked toward the bright sky above them, "it is up there, on the other side, in Heaven."

Skittles tilted her chin upward to gaze at the blue overhead. It was like the blue of the ocean, or the blue of meadow violets, or the blue she saw on the robin's egg in springtime. The sky was beautiful. "Heaven must be a wonderful place, so peaceful and free," Skittles said.

"Oh, it is. It is. No one is hungry or cold or alone in Heaven, and everyone is blessed by God's love," Cat said.

"Then why is Maggie so sad?" Skittles whined. "Shouldn't she be happy for Sammy to go to such a place as that?"

Cat answered, "She's not sad for Sammy, little Skittles. Maggie is sad for herself. Her friend has died, he will never come back, and she misses him. That is why she is sad."

"Then what can I do to help?"

Cat's other eye popped open suddenly and his ears perked up. Something was scurrying through the dirt beneath the barn. "I must go, little Skittles," he said. "There are mice to catch."

Wise Cat had vanished before giving Skittles the answer. But she was sure there must be a way to help Maggie. "I know! We'll go on a journey. We'll have a grand adventure! A change of scenery, that is what Maggie needs, far, far away from that Yearning Tree."

"I don't want to go away. I'm fine right here," Maggie said, barely looking at Skittles.

"But we can have a grand adventure. Think of all the things we can see. Think of all the things we can do," Skittles pleaded.

"There is nothing I want to see or do." Maggie turned her back on Skittles to gaze, once again, at the tree.

Skittles wouldn't give up on her old friend. She tried bossing her. She tried begging her. She tried pestering her day and night. Until...

"All right!" Maggie snapped. "We'll go, if you will only leave me alone."

And the two friends set out—one large, one very small—on their grand adventure.

They crossed ancient mountains.

They waded in the churning sea.

They frolicked in blooming meadows and skipped rocks in trickling streams.

But through it all, as the grand adventure unfolded magnificently all around them, Skittles feared Maggie only pretended to have fun. She caught Maggie constantly looking over her shoulder...

as if the Yearning Tree were always still there.

It was autumn when the friends returned. A season had passed. The journey was behind them, but it had done little good. Maggie was no longer quiet and withdrawn. She was angry.

"Look at it. Just look at it!" Maggie snarled at Skittles; Maggie snarled at the tree.

Skittles looked up at the golden leaves, their edges kissed by dewy sun. She whispered, "I see it. It's the most beautiful tree I've ever seen."

"Beautiful! How can you say it's beautiful? The leaves are dying. See how they fall from the branches?" Maggie shoved past Skittles and stomped across the field.

Skittles looked after her, bewildered.

Night fell and Skittles curled on her bed in the barn alone, shivering. It was chilly, but unlike last fall, Maggie no longer came down from the hill to sleep with her and keep her warm.

"I don't like that tree," Skittles murmured before finally drifting off to sleep.

In her sleep, there came a glorious dream. An angel visited from Heaven. He glowed white like the mist rising off a spring morning's dew with silky flowing hair. He leaned down, down, down to tiny Skittles. In a divine voice made from the sound of rushing rivers and the echoes of forming canyons and the endless sweep of wind through rippling grasslands, he whispered to Skittles the answer. It was the answer she had been seeking all along.

The answer of how to help Maggie.

The tree was bare and gray, its skeletal branches rustling in the frost-bitten wind. Winter had come. Even so, hour after hour, Maggie sat by the tree.

But today, Skittles did what she learned in the dream, and sat with her.

Skittles sat with Maggie the next day...

...and the next...

...until one day, after so very long, a whole year had passed. It was summer again.

For the first time in a great while, Maggie turned her eyes upward, toward the June sky and the tumbles of puffy clouds overhead. Then she looked at Skittles, who had been beside her all along. "It really is a lovely day, isn't it?"

Skittles blinked. It was good to hear her friend's voice. "Yes. A very lovely day."

Maggie nodded. "I bet there are lots of squirrels to chase and rabbits to catch in the woods on a day such as this."

Skittles's tail began to wag excitedly. "Yes, yes!"

"Yes, little one. It is time." Maggie stood up. "Care to join me?"

Maggie took one last look at her tree, and then the two friends—one large and one very small—walked down the hill together.

Maggie and Skittles had many grand adventures after that day, laughing and playing on the farm and beyond. But they still visited the Yearning Tree faithfully, as it stood on the hill year after year.

It was a reminder of those gone, of memories to be cherished, of lifetimes never to be forgotten.

The Yearning Tree was a reminder...

...of love.

This page is dedicated to

_____

Use this blank page for drawing your own special tree (or other memorial) and the loved one you would like to honor.

Discussion Questions

Take a moment to explore these questions and concepts with your child. Remember, there are no wrong answers.

1. Life on the farm is happy for Maggie and Skittles, but then everything changes. What changes?

2. Throughout the story, Skittles refers to the "Yearning Tree." Why do you think she calls the tree by that name? What do you yearn or wish for?

3. Early in the story, Maggie says she is too tired to play with Skittles. Do you think she is physically tired? Mentally? Why do you think she feels this way?

4. What does Wise Cat mean when he says Maggie is not sad for Sammy, she is sad for herself? When have you been sad for yourself and missing a loved one?

5. Skittles encourages Maggie to go on a trip with her. Do you think this was helpful to Maggie? Why or why not?

6.   On the trip, Skittles says she "caught Maggie constantly looking over her shoulder...as if the Yearning Tree were always still there." What does this statement mean? How can a memory follow you?

7.   When autumn comes, the leaves start falling from the Yearning Tree. Why does this seem to make Maggie angry? Is anger a natural reaction to grief? When have you been angry?

8.   In the barn at nighttime, Skittles is lonely and cold. She blames the tree for her feelings, but is Skittles really angry at the tree or something else? Is Maggie hurting Skittles on purpose?

9.   An angel visits Skittles in a dream and gives her the answer as to how to help Maggie. What did the answer turn out to be? How can you be a friend to someone who is sad?

10. The story passes through the seasons and back to summer again. Was the passing of time helpful to Maggie? How can the passing of time heal our hurt feelings?

About the Farago Family

Gina Farago is the award-winning author of two novels, *Ivy Cole and the Moon* and *Luna*, and a Southern cookbook, *Making Do: How to Cook Like a Mountain MeMa*, cowritten with Lois Sutphin. Gina is a former volunteer for Hospice and Palliative Care of Greensboro, N.C., in conjunction with toy poodle Skittles, who is a certified therapy dog through Therapy Dogs International. In addition to Hospice patients, Skittles visits nursing homes and children's camps, spreading joy wherever she goes!

Husband Karl Farago's photographs have graced the covers of *Ivy Cole and the Moon* and *Making Do,* as well as being featured in *Haunted Historic Greensboro* by Theresa Bane. Maggie, a Belgian Malinois and AKC-certified Canine Good Citizen, is the second love of his life!

Lightning Source UK Ltd.
Milton Keynes UK
UKHW051956090123
415088UK00002B/9